Cut From A Different Kente

J. Scott

Table of Contents

Opening Prayer

"New beginnings big or small, Lord I pray you bless them all. Thank you for Your day, and grace, for my people make a way. Hoping that they know the time, it's time to rise, and time to grind.

Who I Am

Mama's not doing well, Daddy's not here
I feel alone, I have no cheer
I do have friends, I do have fam
I should thank God for who I am
I am intelligent, I love to read
I shine bright, in the darkness of the sea
(lighthouse)
I am a bearer of good news and cheer
It's my time, as I look in the mirror

Who I Am

This poem was derived from the perspective of friends, and family I grew up with, and what I wish we all knew to stay strong throughout our childhood. I grew up in a poor-middle class neighborhood. I hated looking in the mirror because I saw my friends and their struggles within vme. I went to church every Week, but I lacked a relationship with God which led to depression, and caused me to suffer. I feel like "Who I Am" is a great motivational poem to motivate people battling with depression, who have been through(or are currently going though) what I went through as a young man.

Peace Be Still

Still I rise through the triumphs
Still I rise through the lows
If you can't rise above
You're on a downward slope
Sometimes all we need is water
Sometimes all we need is love
I pray that peace be still
I don't have another rush
A rush to judgement, a rush to hatred
A rush to love, a rush to lust
I've mustered all the strength I have
To turn my life into a just
What's in store, is so much more
Patience is a virtue
I refuse to be a wordsmith
Out of spite to hurt you
Still I rise, just to nurture, because our
Mother is getting old

Still I rise, for my Father, because I'll never
sell my soul
Still I rise for His people
In His image we're alike
Hope you see me through my soul
Hope you see you in your light

Peace Be Still

"Peace Be Still" is about being aware of your trials and tribulations. Don't live an artificial life. Slow down, think, and do what's best for you. Rise above your mental aptitude to become successful in your own way. Reserve your energy for what's important to you, and don't waste your physical, or spiritual currency.

I Am Well

I am well, crossed troubled waters
No one man crew, together we do
We love as ours, many moons ago
No moor, no less than that
We face a troubled path often
Every atom plays his/her role
Don't wander from storms, no please
don't scurry
Please don't stray from the trials of
the tribe
Though yours aren't mine
We work towards the greater good
For all mankind we connect through a
flower
Such a delicate way from destruction

I Am Well

I wrote this poem, when I first got to the hospital at the end of black history month. One of my mentors told me about a sacred geometry symbol called flower of life. This poem to me is an interpretation of the meaning. My belief about the universe is that everyone/everything works together for the greater good, and how fragile that peace is. The gospel song "I need you to survive" is a theme.

Martin Luther

Martin had a dream, he also had a vision
He also had a plan, he also had a mission
Try to find your worth, in a purpose that is
driven
You can be the driver, or simply pitch in
Becoming one's own, doesn't mean you
have to start a business
It's finding your purpose
Merchant or preacher, we all play a role
Construct your heart inward, stand tall
break the mold

Martin Luther

This poem is a mixture about Martin Luther, who brought the printing press to the world allowing texts(especially the Bible) to be spread, and Martin Luther King. It helped me with my own pride. I humble myself, and my ego, through my writings. I speak from the heart, read it again, and correct the errors in my ways because I'm not a hypocrite. I have much more work to do on myself, to be the best person I can be. For myself, and the struggle.

Make Your Mark

Make your mark, set a tone
Write goals down, etched in stone
Care for yourself because our world is
cruel
Never stop learning, do your best in school
Cool is being smart, intelligent, poised
Girls, they love those kind of boys
Boys, they love those kind of girls
Live your best life, and shape your world

Make Your Mark

"Make Your Mark" isn't about becoming monetarily successful. It's about making a mark affecting the lives of others in a positive way.

Sportsmanship

Play with pride, play to win
Practice makes us perfectly imperfect
Perfect your craft, put in the work
We don't have to be perfect, just be
prepared
Like the food on your table that
nourishes you
Learn from your loved ones, and flourish
in truth
A loss isn't losing, take lessons from L's
Enjoy your experience, you're gonna
prevail

Sportsmanship

"Sportsmanship" is about persevering in life in general, not just sports. It's about preparing for the road ahead of you. Life is hard, and we all have obstacles to overcome. We ARE perfectly imperfect.

Somebody Loves You

Look in the mirror, and love who you see
God made an original, reflection of me
Sometimes we can't see the good
Through our faults and flaws
But our story to tell, can't reside in
these walls
Someone needs the encouragement,
quiet as kept
Step out on your faith, that lies in the
depths
Turn what's inward outward for the
world to see
Because what's inward relates to what
resides in me

Somebody Loves You

There was a time when I looked in the mirror when I was battling depression. I looked in the mirror and said "who are you". I was lost trying to find myself in the psych ward, and I couldn't even recognize the man in the mirror. I wrote this poem to uplift others, and let it be known that I've been in that dark place before, and can relate. This poem is for people battling depression, and also an uplifting poem about huemility that all people can relate to. You are an original reflection of me.

No Stars

No stars in the sky
A breeze gentle as I search and desire
Fortunate knights, a place in God's riddle
Time taken, no time lost, to build what's
sacred
Peace of mind I speak of
A wisdom gained through the flame
A dire need to be sane, I dropped the
ball Lord
Help me, God I need you through
these days
Big words don't lift my spirit
I have faith lesser than most
Life eating at my soul
But it's Your presence, and Your Helper
Please O Lord just make me whole

No Stars

This poem is about accepting the complexity of life, and choosing to acknowledge my individual quest of God's riddle that can't be solved. It's about having the peace of mind to share with others my insecurities, and to be open and optimistic about struggles I went/ go through. It's about staying humble, and being honest about the struggle of everyday people as we search and desire for more. It's about not being ashamed to not have your life together, or having all the answers to life that we seek.

Down and Out

Been down and out to long, it's time for us to rise
No depression, life's a blessing, now it's time to dry your eyes
In the mirror, hope it's clearer, in his image we're alike
You deserve to know your worth
Hope you see you through my sight,
Hope you see you through your light, dark days, we make it through them
I don't do this for myself, I'm stronger trying to speak for you
When money won't mean much, trust, if I can't lift your spirit
I struggle too, but love will do, through the lows, it lifts my spirit
We might be down, but we serve an on time God

He never counts us out, we'll win against
the odds
Strive and struggle to prosper, invest in
your down time
No spirit of fear, of power, love, and a
sound mind

Down And Out

The beginning of this poem was originally a verse to a song I wrote. I wanted to uplift people who can't see their worth, and see them through the lense that I see through.. I cherish the connections I have with my loved ones, and have been through some dark days, trials, and tribulations. I believe that God works through people sometimes, and everyone deserves to be uplifted, especially through their trials, and tribulations. I believe in seeing our likeness as opposed to our differences when it comes to different cultures. That is what brings us together. When you can see me in you, and you in me, that is what changes the world for the better.

Builder of Faith

Builder of faith, Lover of my Soul
Keeper of the covenants, the One who
made me whole
We live to serve your purpose, the naked
shall be clothed
Our tests are meant to help another, pride
we set aside
A poor man's dream we once had, now
spiritual wealth we seek
Out of darkness, into the light, your word it
is to lead
Your gift by grace, is everlasting abounded
to who believes
By faith we're saved, and give you praise,
for that gift from you to me

Builder of Faith

This poem is about striving to be a better
person. Once you accept that we are
righteous by faith, you should want to be
a better person. God is a keeper of his
covenant, which is a builder of the faithful.
I wrote this poem because wanting to be
financially wealthy led me to depression
when we should seek spiritual wealth in
doing right by others, and cherishing God's
graciousness and mercy working in our
lives.

Washed

Birds chirping, over the sunrise bloom
Other queer sounds, as morning resumes
A newfangled walk down memory lane
What's old, what's new, both one in
the same
Good times, these memoirs
Of steps once taken
Bathed in beauty, with nurtured placement
A beauty divine, a sight to see
The world really doesn't revolve around me

Washed

This poem was written one morning as I walked through the neighborhood I grew up in early one morning reminiscing about the good times, the bad times, and enjoying all the memories and sounds around me. Bathing in the beauty of nature cleansed my spirit, and helped me share my experience with you.

Four square

Four square is more than a ball and a drive
It's freedom expressed wherewithal in
your eyes
It's fun and a game, if you accept the
challenge
Sportsmanship it is wherewithal in your
balance
Honest and just, carried in the right
manner
Exercise your thoughts, the Lord is our
banner

Four square

This poem was a double entendre about a game I grew up playing in the driveway of our yards growing up,, and a new meaning I found while reading the dictionary about expressing yourself. Express your opinion in a respectful way, and stand on your square. Are you ready?

Keepsake

Cherish your memories, good and the bad
Connect with your loved ones, remember
the past
Life is everlasting, though rivers may flow
Wade in the water, then you will find
strength
Deep down inside, understanding will
surface
Take time and love on your loved ones it's
worth it

Keepsake

This poem is about cherishing your memories of your loved ones whether it's through video, a year book, photographs, or good times stored in your memory bank. Remember where you came from, who you are, and where you're headed. Cherish the memories you create, and take the good from every situation and grow from them. Enjoy time with your loved ones.

When In Doubt

When in doubt, search for strength
It's deep within your being
A treasure worth no price at all(priceless)
In the mirror, is what you're seeing
A gift from God, a new day awaits
Love yourself and smile today.

When In Doubt

This poem was meant for an early morning tooth brush, face cloth, or shower experience for people of all ages. It's about recognizing your worth as you embark upon the day's journey. When in doubt, smile and see the beauty in your reflection. It's worth it.

Hypnotic

I will not become victim, to depression's
hypnotic rhythm
Steady drifting because my vision really
isn't purpose driven
The seductions of this world can lead
astray any day
So many complexities in this matrix we
call life
It could all be so simple, but what isn't
simple is my sinful nature that goes against
who? My Creator
Because my heart and my mind, won't
align with my spine, or my soul, or my
spirit
But you know, you can feel it
But my purpose as a wordsmith is to
sow,not to fear this
See my strength through my weakness
To change my hypnotic sequence
Reality is we don't have forever
But we do have today, to change our
rhythm for the better

Hypnotic

This poem is about the power of habits, and forming proper habits that will make you successful in life. The first step is recognizing our flaws, and how we can fix our rhythms for the better by forming new habits, and improving on our good habits. This poem was originally a spoken word poem that I wanted to share in this collection of poems. When I wrote this poem I was fed up with my current situation, and wanted to express myself, and show my overcomer's spirit for others to help build someone else through my life's journey. It was a turning point in my life not to get stuck in my current situation, and continue striving to be the best person I could be through my learning experience.

R x R

We are righteous by faith, not righteous by
reason
Rest and relax, extract from the season
Find your North Star, or purpose in life
Purposefully drive onward and upward
Influence others through actions
and words
Don't fail your tests, testify on this earth
Helping another's worth more than a dollar
Walk in those shoes, and just walk toward
tomorrow
How can you wander a path never taken
Take that to heart, history in the making

R x R

This rest and relaxation play on words is about removing yourself from your situation, and understanding that a purpose driven life may lead to a road not taken. "You can't walk a mile in my shoes" is a very famous quote. I believe that is how we gain understanding. Acknowledging another person's situation is what helps us grow as a human race. Take that walk, listen, and learn. Maybe then it will be your turn.

North Star

As I search for peace and guidance
Lead a purpose driven way
I can't wander any longer
Not tomorrow, nor today
I don't have but too much longer
Patience is a virtue, and crutch
I value time, I value love
Hypnotic Rhythm is a must
As I lay me down to sleep
I pray the Lord my soul to keep
Give of me, give of thee
Helping people on their feet
Any way that we can do
You and me, me and you

North Star

This poem is simply about putting your
faith and trust in God. One of my purposes
is to uplift others. It is confirmation that I
want God to use me for a higher purpose if
it is in His will.

Trottin' Not Forgotten

Stampede! Stampede!
I'm just taking my time
Simply put, I'm not swift, I'm steady
I'm staying out of the way of the fast
paced race
I'm more like the tortoise than the hare
Wind breezing through my hair, I'm
enjoying the pace
Don't think I'll be finishing first
Which is alright because my friends will
That is alright with me
I'm just trottin' not forgotten
I remember this trail
I need to take my time
Time waits for no man, but patience is
the key
As the world turns, lead don't follow me

Trottin' Not Forgotten

I wrote this poem when I was battling depression for people going through a similar situation. It's about accepting things I cannot change, and wishing the best for my friends and family. I'm pray for the success of all my loved ones, and I know I am not forgotten. I value relationships, and the connections I have with others. Moving towards my purpose has led to many trials and tribulations, and ups and downs. I have lost loved ones, and know how it feels to feel alone and forgotten. This poem is about having the strength to continue the race called life.

Network Theory (Hippocampus)

Time will not break our constellation
Every memory is a node in series or
parallel
Some memories I can't store for growth
No rhyme scheme needed, free verse
where I failed
I'm a winner who lost, was a boy
not a man
But I have enough favor from God
within me
To show who I am, I am not that man

Network Theory (Hippocampus)

This free verse poem is about my time in college when I lost my way. I was studying to be an electrical engineer, but my classes got too hard for me to pass, and I got kicked out of school. Life was difficult, I didn't know how to rebuild my life, and I was depressed. It also goes along with "Trottin' Not Forgotten" and how I still value the connections and friends I made while I was in school. I'm proud of all my friends and family who were able to graduate. If anyone has been through a similar situation, I hope this explanation helps you in your journey.

Walk This Way

Chin up, chest out, walk with confidence
They may not flatter, they may not
compliment
Don't walk too proud, or hang your head
Things could be worse, accept your
situation
Don't run from problems, don't run at all
Stand on your square, whether short or tall
Show your drive, don't take a backseat
It's your life to live, and you only have one

Walk This Way

This poem is about having the confidence to continue striving and achieving. Whether you have to switch careers, overcome obstacles, or overcome stressful situations, you can do it. Running from my problems was one of my biggest mistakes in my twenties. It leads to wandering down a dark road. Be the light in this world through Christ who strengthens us.

Essence

She is beautiful
Essence like poetry
Lovers ever more

Essence

This is a haiku I wrote about love and to uplift people in relationships. We all know the beauty of poetry, and how all the different forms of poetry has shaped our world for the better.

Silhouette

Shadow against the night time walls
No apparel, about to spark
I saved a dance from me to you
Are you afraid of the dark?

Silhouette

This poem is about intimacy in a poetic/ mature way.

The Womb

A woman is respected on both ends of the
spectrum
The nexus of creation
A symbol now mistaken
Tradition counterclockwise
Once upon, turned into hatred
Never lessen your true beauty
Knowledge is power

The Womb

The womb is about the African swastika, and how it was turned into a symbol for hate. The symbol has many positive connotations in many cultures in the past. Research what is hidden.

Touch Of A Woman

The Midas touch can't compare to the
touch of a woman
The real architects of life, men, we just like
to fight
Our protectors from the womb, which a
house is built on
I believe in Patriachs, but what about the
Matriachs?
Providing has been misconstrued to
represent money
That's an empirical formula, the base of the
pyramid
Women are the eye, without life isn't worth
living
If I was blind, I'd still see your worth
I'd still sense your value, I'd still feel your
warmth, I'd still hear your voice,
I'd still feel love and compassion, I'd still
taste victory in compliment, the symmetry
of our hearts

Touch Of A Woman

There is nothing more powerful in this
world than love. I wrote this poem for
all the Queens who are heads of their
households, and families, to let them
know they are appreciated. I also wrote
this poem when I was lonely, dreaming to
have the touch of a woman, and seeing a
woman's worth.

Storm Chasers

We tend to run towards trouble, thinking
we'll be good
Then suffer consequences not
intended for us
Suffering isn't God's plan
He gave us free will, since the first Adam

Storm Chasers

God doesn't cause suffering in our lives.
Being a man who has caused suffering in
my life through my own faults and flaws,
I just wanted to share this poem out of
maturity that I have caused problems that I
wouldn't have had to go through if I chose
to be more mature in my early years. It's
never too late to change our ways for our
betterment.

Love Runs

Love is deeper than any well
Love surpasses unjust thought
Love is not law, love is felt
Love is built, trust is formed
From that trust you cannot run

Love Runs

The title to this poem was inspired by a good friend of mine who ran track in high school, and college. This poem is about coexistence between cultures, and the complexities of keeping peace in the world. It's also about the strength and bonds of families, and close friends.

Greater Good

The greater good in my own way
Is what I seek, and what I pray
It's why I strive, and why I build
To connect with others, that's how I feel
God is good, no God is great
I pray the Lord my soul to take
To rest in You, through my dreams
No one man band, we are a team

Greater Good

I saved this poem for the end of my book to let it be known God is God all alone. He uses who he wants to, and I've asked him to use me to uplift others. I am thankful for the ideas, and allowing me to go through the creative process of bring this poem book to fruition through my struggles. Hopefully my words will inspire and uplift all communities, not just the black community.

Made in the USA
Middletown, DE
26 February 2023

25360442R00035